CW00730056

Pentecostalism

From a Catholic perspective

by
Dr Cyprian Blamires

All booklets are published thanks to the
generous support of the members of the
Catholic Truth Society

CATHOLIC TRUTH SOCIETY
PUBLISHERS TO THE HOLY SEE

Contents

A huge phenomenon of our time

The wildfire growth of the Pentecostal Movement in many parts of the world today is one of the most impressive features of Christian history since the end of World War II. Pentecostalism has made huge inroads in many areas long considered bastions of the Catholic Church – such as Latin America – as well as in many other parts of the world such as Africa south of the Sahara and notably in South Korea. The largest local church in the world, in Seoul, is a Pentecostalist church claiming membership of over 800,000. But what exactly is this exploding Pentecostalism and how should we respond to it as Catholics?

The Day of Pentecost

The term 'Pentecostalist' derives from the word 'Pentecost' as in the Day of Pentecost. The Day of Pentecost as described in the Book of Acts was a day of extraordinary and spectacular miracles, a day of huge excitement and energy which has been traditionally interpreted as a unique outpouring of God's Holy Spirit, made visible to the human eye in the tongues of fire that hovered over the heads of those present, made audible to the human ear in the sound of a rushing mighty wind, made powerful to the mind in the miraculous ability of all the individuals in the polyglot gathering suddenly to understand each others' language. Pentecostalism is only the most recent and the most modern of many many movements all down the history of the Church which have looked at the reports of the happenings on the Day of Pentecost and wanted to rediscover or recreate not only the excitement of that day, but also the dynamism and miracle-filled life of those first early stages in the life of the Church that followed it as recorded in the Book of Acts.

The life of miracles

Generation after generation of Christians has included those with a sense of disappointment at the seemingly routine nature of much of Church life as compared with the diet of miracles and extraordinary phenomena that prevailed in the first days of the life of the Church.

Generation after generation of Christians has thrown up individuals convinced that the life of miracles could become normal fare for the Church of their day. It is into just this category that Pentecostalists fall. They are people who lay claim to be living proof of the continuing prevalence of miracles and extraordinary phenomena as normal features of the Christian life in the modern age.

Belief and practice

A considerable part of what Pentecostalists believe and practise in areas such as the role of the Bible and spontaneity in liturgy is also believed and practised by adherents of the Evangelical Protestant movement which gave birth to Pentecostalism, while another part in areas such as 'the baptism in the Spirit' and speaking in tongues is believed and practised by followers of the Charismatic Movement, who are found in most of the denominations as well as in the Catholic Church. So it is important to understand how Pentecostalists are different from these two other global movements.

Pentecostalists - a subgroup among Evangelicals

Virtually all Pentecostal denominations and sects originally emerged out of the broader Evangelical movement, of which they are a kind of subgroup – even though many of their Evangelical peers down the years have regarded them with suspicion or even with downright hostility. So first of all it is necessary to explain what Evangelicalism is.

Evangelicalism

Evangelical religion itself represents a particular subgroup or subculture within global Protestantism – and an exceedingly powerful one. Evangelicals are often known today as 'born-again Christians'. They are also variously known by terms such as 'Hot Gospellers', 'Bible Christians', 'Fundamentalists' or even less politely as 'Bible Bashers'. They stand out among Protestants at large on account of their great reverence for the Bible text as the written word of God and their desire to find guidance in it for every part of their lives.

A personal conversion experience

They are known for their strong emphasis on the need for everyone to undergo a personal conversion experience –

'Ye must be born again' as Our Lord said. To this end they support and promote a great number of evangelistic outreach programmes and events designed to draw individuals into 'giving their lives to Christ' as they see it.

'The altar call'

The focus on these occasions is often on what has traditionally been known as 'the altar call' – the climax of the gathering, when, having given a summary of what he or she understands to be the core of the gospel, the preacher or minister invites individuals present to signify their desire to commit themselves to Jesus then and there and on the spot by coming to the front and receiving a blessing, or simply by joining him or her (in fact it is usually a 'him') in a simple prayer of commitment. Once they have made such a commitment in their minds or by saying an appropriate prayer out loud, the crusade leader invites them to join a local 'bible-believing' (i.e. Evangelical) worshipping community in order to develop their faith further.

The classic example of this type of public crusade evangelism in recent years was that of the Billy Graham Crusades – a tradition continued by younger evangelists today whose names however are nothing like as well-known as Graham's. For several decades after World War II, Billy Graham drew vast crowds to his evangelistic rallies all over the world, and his name became instantly recognisable to vast numbers of people: indeed, he was for several decades the best known Evangelical across the globe.

Preaching and ordinance

Evangelicals place a great emphasis on preaching as a means of sharing the gospel, though they also make use of theatricals and bands singing sacred songs – which they refer to as 'Christian music'. Evangelical worship consists mainly of sacred songs, extempore prayer, and fervent bible-based preaching, with liturgical actions generally pared to a minimum. The architecture of their church buildings is usually plain and simple, the focus is on the lectern or podium or pulpit, the place where the preaching is done. Often today rock bands lead the music and in the Megachurches (a term generally used for a local church which has a Sunday attendance of more than 2000 or so) there may be massed robed choirs but the preacher usually wears a suit or sometimes a plain gown.

'The Lord's Supper' is celebrated at varying intervals but certainly not daily and it does not have the central importance that the mass has in the daily life of the Catholic Church. It often involves consumption of non-alcoholic or unfermented wine. It is more likely to be regarded as 'an ordinance' rather than as a sacrament.

Personal relationship with Jesus

What Evangelicals are perhaps most famous for is their idea of the Christian faith as 'a personal relationship with God'. They hold this idea in common with many other non-Evangelical Christians – including many of the Catholic saints – something they have been generally reluctant to recognise. What this means for them is a frequent spontaneous conversation with God during their waking hours, asking God's guidance in all their decision-making, and applying bible texts in daily life. Often this translates into a particularly noticeable use of words – 'The Lord led me to do such-and-such' is a classic Evangelical expression, trying to convey that a particular action was taken in the belief that it was directly commanded from above.

The Holy Spirit

The extension of the idea of 'living by faith' in daily life into such areas as choosing a marriage partner can have dramatic results. Stories abound for example of individuals who have prayed for a partner and gone out and seen someone they believed to be 'the Lord's choice' for them, ending up with a marriage proposal on the spot.

Decisions may often be taken on the strength of a supposed 'message from the Lord', while rational planning and reflection can often be considered inferior to 'openness to the Spirit' sometimes with a rather disappointing end product, classically in the matter of sermons and talks.

The carefully planned and structured homily may give way to an outpouring under the 'reliance on the Spirit' that does not match up to expectations. Such behaviour is in fact particularly characteristic of Pentecostalists. They are especially prone to avoiding a 'common-sense' or 'rational' approach to the decisions of daily life with what seems to them to be a direct dependence on the Holy Spirit.

The present author recalls a discussion with a Pentecostalist many years ago in which he had the temerity to offer a different perspective from that of the Pentecostalist on some matter or other. 'Who are you to question what the Holy Spirit has told me?' was the tart conversation-stopper. Individuals can often be tempted to use what they perceive to be their direct inspiration by the Holy Spirit to close out arguments and shut the mouths of opponents. The role of the Holy Spirit is crucial in Pentecostalism, which could almost be defined as 'the religion of the Holy Spirit'.

No single church

One big feature of Evangelical religion is the bewildering variety of sects into which it is divided, and this is a characteristic feature of Pentecostalism as well. Evangelicals have a very weak sense of ecclesial discipline and are liable to take off and start new movements or communities of believers if they feel that the one to which they belong is not loyal enough to the message of Scripture or in some cases, simply 'not lively enough'.

Sometimes avowed Christian believers stop attending any form of public worship, claiming to be unable to find a church that is 'true to Scripture'. 'Christ is the answer, not the Church' is a classic slogan of Evangelical preachers, or 'not religion but Jesus'. They tend to see the churches as a kind of 'necessary evil', masking the true face of Christ with their sinfulness rather than revealing it, whereas that face shines infallibly through the pages of the Bible. A typical contrast made by preachers is one between *'Christ-ianity'* and *'Church-ianity'*.

Revivalism

Many Evangelical preachers and writers long for the outbreak of what is known as 'Revival'. In this they have in mind specific periods of Protestant history when a great spirit of religious excitement and fervour of devotion gripped whole communities. In the US two such periods were known as the Great Awakenings, in the UK the Welsh Revival at the start of the twentieth century is often quoted.

Catholic history is of course also peppered with stories of a similar kind – events around the tomb of Deacon Paris caused great controversy among the Jansenists in the eighteenth century, for example, while similar excitement was generated around the more mainstream Catholic St Louis Grignon de Montfort with his missions. Certain of such revivals were characterised by outbreaks of some of the typically Pentecostalist or charismatic phenomena.

The Welsh Revivals

The Welsh Revivals of 1859 and 1904-5 have a particular place in the mythology of Pentecostalism. The latter took its rise in West Wales and involved a number of significant manifestations, including tongues-speaking. A great spirit of penitence was observed, affecting church members and drawing in converts. This spirit of penitence led to outbursts of weeping in public worship. The normal structures of services and the time limits were abandoned and worship went on for hours.

Rediscovering ecstatic experience

In essence, what we have is classic ecstatic experiences – people gathered together simply forgot themselves and their surroundings and the normal framework governing their church activity and got caught up in a kind of rapture. This is something that many people crave – to be taken out of themselves, so that they forget time and place as if with a kind of foretaste of eternity. Pentecostalism is of all the Protestant movements the most revivalistic, the most concerned with rediscovering the ecstatic experiences recorded among believers in the past.

The emergence of modern Pentecostalism

The modern Pentecostal movement is usually considered to have begun at the beginning of the twentieth century in the US, when worshippers at a meeting at the African Methodist Episcopal Church in Los Angeles in 1906 were gifted with tongues-speaking in a context of inter-racial mingling.

Pastor Joseph Smale

A Los Angeles pastor named Joseph Smale had gone to Wales to see the revival for himself and preached about it on his return to the US. Thereafter reports of worship services accompanied by miraculous healings, tongues-speaking, and lifestyle conversions began to spread across America.

William J Seymour

William J Seymour, son of a former slave, was preaching that the baptism of the Holy Spirit was accompanied with speaking in tongues. He and a small group of followers prayed for this 'baptism of the Holy Spirit', which they eventually received in April 1906.

The Azusa Street building into which they moved attracted large numbers of worshippers of different races, an unusual feature at the time, as was the encouragement given to women's leadership. Worship was frequent and continuous and attracted individuals from various denominations.

A contemporary newspaper report described them as working themselves into 'a state of mad excitement', characterised the noise they made as 'howlings', and noted that they claimed the gift of tongues. One observer reported that

> 'they run, jump, shake all over, shout to the top of their voice, spin round in circles, fall out on the sawdust blanketed floor jerking, kicking, and rolling all over it. Some of them pass out and do not move for hours as though they were dead … They claim to be filled with the Spirit'.

William Seymour was a disciple of Charles Parham who had been preaching the importance of speaking in tongues as a sign of the baptism of the Holy Spirit since 1901. The Los Angeles press took a great interest in the events on Azusa Street and other similar gatherings began to be held further afield. Most of the main Pentecostal denominations can trace their origins back to this place and time.

Fissuring

All varieties of Protestantism are prone to fissuring, and Pentecostalism has perhaps been the worst at this. In common with the Baptists, Pentecostalists practised believers' baptism by immersion as the norm, and one particularly prominent division arose over the idea that baptism should be 'in the name of Jesus' only. The anti-Trinitarian sects that resulted became known as 'the Oneness Movement'.

What sets the Pentecostalists apart from other Evangelicals?

There are a number of classic features of Pentecostalist worship that separate it from typical Evangelical and other Protestant styles of worship. The most famous of these is, as we have seen, tongues-speaking. It can take two forms. It can issue as a language unknown to speaker and to hearers alike. At other times it issues as an unfamiliar language different from that of the worship service, and another worshipper present may claim to be able to interpret or translate it.

Traditionally it is for this tongues-speaking above all that Pentecostal worship has been famous and it is a practice regarded with suspicion by non-Pentecostal Evangelical churches. There is in addition a similar phenomenon known as 'singing in tongues'.

Tongue-speaking in public worship

The outbreaks of tongues-speaking and other 'ecstatic' behaviour during Evangelical worship services in Los

Angeles at the start of the twentieth century were typically met with hostility and rejection by the leadership of the worshipping communities concerned, which was what led to the establishment of separate communities that eventually acquired the label of 'Pentecostal'.

Tongues-speaking in public worship thus defined the essential difference between 'Pentecostal' and other Protestant worship communities from the start – along with the accompanying phenomena such as people falling prostrate, leaping up and down, embracing one another or even laughing uncontrollably. Forced to choose between indulging their tongues-speaking and other unconventional activities in a public worship setting and their membership of their worshipping communities, the individuals concerned chose to leave and set up fresh separate movements.

Baptism in the Spirit: the fault line between traditional Evangelicals and Pentecostalists

The phenomena of tongues-speaking and the other ecstatic experiences associated with it are closely bound up with the idea of 'baptism in the Spirit'. Fundamental to Pentecostalism is the idea that water baptism must be followed up at some point in the life of the believer by 'baptism in the Spirit'.

In the experience of the baptism of the Spirit the believer receives the gifts of the Spirit whether the gift of tongues-speaking or the gift of prophecy or the gift of healing or some other – as described for example in 1 Corinthians 12, 8-11. The meaning of the expression has been much disputed.

Pentecostalists insist that there is another baptism separate from water baptism, which consists in an outpouring of the Holy Spirit into the heart of the believer. Whereas water baptism consists of an outward sacramental action without any external signs, baptism in the Spirit involves the endowment of the believer with gifts of the Spirit - such as tongues-speaking/interpretation of tongues or prophecy or healing.

The precise nature of this baptism in the Spirit and its position in the life of the believer is a subject of controversy within Pentecostalism itself. There are those sects for example who claim that the experience is an essential part of the life of the Christian, others for whom it may be regarded as an extra for individuals.

The teaching that there is a special baptism of the spirit available to all believers now today as before in the past is one that separates Pentecostalists from more traditional Evangelicals and it remains a source of great controversy among them. The most trenchant critiques and exposés of Pentecostalist beliefs and claims actually come from their fellow Evangelical believers.

Divine healing

Among the gifts of the Spirit is healing, and this after tongues-speaking is a very particular characteristic of the Pentecostalist movement. Again, it is far from being unique to that movement, it is found across the Protestant denominations and is an essential part of Catholic practice as well.

The Catholic approach is exemplified for example in the life of St Pio of Pietrelcina – or Padre Pio as he is still remembered – who possessed a special healing gift. But he also greatly respected scientific medicine and promoted the construction of a hospital close to his friary. There are stories of Pentecostalists so imbued with the importance of the idea of divine healing that they are reluctant to allow traditional medical or surgical interventions.

Television broadcasts

For Pentecostalism, divine healing is often the heart and centre of the regular worship experience, rather than being an occasional feast. A Pentecostalist service or meeting will classically involve the preacher or worship leader inviting the sick to come up to the podium for healing, and this kind of event can be seen regularly on television broadcasts on stations like God TV or Inspiration TV and the like.

One broadcasting station, TBN (Trinitarian Bible Network), is currently owned by a Pentecostalist and it has Spanish, Russian, Italian, and European frequencies on which it hosts programmes broadcast, for example, from branches of the Hillsong community based in Sydney, Australia.

A personality cult

At the time of writing, alongside the Pastor of this community his wife is also deeply involved in the church leadership, and this is a reminder of a curious feature of Pentecostalist churches: they seem frequently not only to involve husband-and-wife teams, but even to encourage a dynastic transfer of leadership which goes from father to son or sometimes to daughter. Such was the case for example with the church founded by the legendary American preacher Aimee Semple McPherson, the International Foursquare gospel church - who was succeeded in the pastorate by her son Rolf McPherson.

This is fully in line with the tendency to a personality cult which often attaches to the temples of Pentecostalism. Once again, however, the same tendency has often been seen in traditional Evangelicalism, from the likes of John Wesley and George Whitfield down to Billy Graham and Rick Warren, pastor of the Saddleback Megachurch in Lake Forest, California (a high-profile preacher and writer cultivated by US politicians) and John Stott, for several decades after World War II the uncrowned king of the English Evangelical movement.

'Slain in the Spirit'

These televised services and meetings also nowadays feature a curious phenomenon which is said to represent a mysterious experience referred to by St Paul with the expression 'slain in the Spirit'. As individuals approach the preacher on the dais, he either touches them on the forehead or simply points his hand towards them and they collapse there and then.

The expression 'slain in the Spirit' does not occur in the Bible but of course there are several references to individuals falling before God in fear and reverence – as the disciples did at the Transfiguration. In Pentecostalist services it is not uncommon for individual worshippers to lie on the floor for longer or shorter periods.

In the Miracle Crusades held regularly by the celebrated evangelist Benny Hinn (from an Orthodox family, educated in Catholic Schools), he has a habit of throwing out his hand towards individuals on the stage who usually collapse, and it seems that this is in some way regarded as an act of imparting the Spirit and part of the process of alleged healing. It is important to say 'alleged', because doubts have been raised repeatedly about the so-called 'miracle cures' performed by evangelists like Hinn. Studies have shown that some who were apparently 'cured' in fact relapsed into their afflicted state soon after. Real healing cannot be ascertained overnight but needs time to prove itself.

Addictive laughter

Another phenomenon typical of these events is that of prolonged outbursts of laughter as individuals find themselves gripped by an uncontrollable desire to giggle. This is often provoked by the minister appealing to the sense of joy in the congregants as to what the Lord has done for them and what he plans for them. Even more outlandish phenomena have been reported in connection with such events such as people barking like dogs or making other strange noises.

Pentecostal denominations and congregations

Confusingly, many Pentecostal denominations or sects do not identify themselves as such by their names. 'Elim church' is a popular designation, this has a biblical reference, for Elim was a place the Israelites came to in the course of their Exodus from Egypt which had an abundance of wells and date palms.

'Foursquare gospel church' is another: the term refers to the four doctrines of salvation, the presence of the Holy Spirit, healing, and millennialism. Millennialism – based on the idea of a millennium – i.e. a thousand years, is the belief that the last judgement will be preceded by a paradisal thousand-year period on earth. There is a strong current among Pentecostalists, incidentally, that expects the second coming of Christ in the present generation. But there are innumerable different names for Pentecostalist communities.

One of the best known and largest is the World Assemblies of God Fellowship, with 300,000 congregations worldwide and a claimed membership pushing 60 million. On the other hand there are denominations like Revival Centres International based in Australia, which has around 300 fellowships in 22 countries, where the choice of the term 'revival' is suggestive of what is felt to be the meaning and purpose of the work.

The birthday of the Church for Catholics

For Catholics, the Day of Pentecost (previously known as Whitsunday or Whitsun) is treasured above all as the birthday of the Church. The New Testament book of the Acts of the Apostles tells us that on that day Christ, whose earthly body had ascended to heaven shortly before, returned in the Spirit, no longer held captive within the bounds of matter, and entered right into the depths of the hearts and lives of his followers.

A rushing mighty wind was heard by the assembled band and then tongues of fire danced through the room and individuals began to speak in other languages. Each understood all the others, something which was symbolic of the breaking down of barriers between races and nations that was to be a feature of the life of the Church.

It was also a reversal of what happened with the fall of the Tower of Babel, when men's pride was punished by the introduction of language barriers between them. The little band became the Body of Christ, and that Body extended from that day all down history and all over the world, it is the Body into which believers today are incorporated in baptism.

A day of miracles for Pentecostalists

Although most Pentecostalists would also refer to the Day of Pentecost as the birthday of the Church (while of course they can only use this word in a metaphorical sense, as a term to refer to all believers, since they have no single Church but only a multitude of denominations and congregations) – for them the Day of Pentecost is in reality above all about miracles.

It is about the experience of the Holy Spirit making his presence felt in the form of extraordinary phenomena: speaking in tongues, mysterious flames of fire, a rushing mighty wind. Miraculous healings, prophecies, ecstatic experiences, Pentecostalists claim that this kind of experience, far from being a unique unrepeatable moment in the history of the Church, can be and ought to be part of the everyday life of ordinary believers now today.

What they want is for Church life today to be a repeat of the life of the first Christians as recorded in the Acts of the Apostles, complete with miracles of healing, prophecies, and 'tongues-speaking'. Curiously, this attitude – though typically finding expression in all the clothing of modernity in terms of the use of modern media such as the television and the internet and contemporary rock music - represents a desire to return to the past; for the days of the Early Church are as a matter of fact long gone, and modern movements can hope to recapture only something of their spirit. Some Protestant apologists have in any case in the past claimed that miracles were only ever intended by God as a necessary fuel to launch the Church on her way, and that miracles died out because they were no longer necessary.

Benny Hinn and the 'Miracle Crusades'

It is not for nothing that Benny Hinn, one of the foremost Pentecostalist preachers and evangelists at the present time (his internationally aired TV programmes are said to be among the most-watched 'Christian programmes' on TV today), calls his sessions 'Miracle Crusades'.

It seems clear that what motivates Pentecostalism is the thirst for miracles – in other words, the longing to see God's power demonstrated *conclusively* by divine interference in the natural order of things. Healings, prophecies, tongues-speaking, being 'slain in the Spirit', addictive laughter, etc are all extraordinary phenomena even if they may not necessarily qualify as 'miraculous'.

It is easily overlooked that the longing to see the power of God visibly and unmistakably at work in extraordinary supernatural phenomena is not a sign of exceptional faith, but in fact a symptom of doubt. Those who put their trust in Christ crucified and grow in faith and love and devotion *without* witnessing or experiencing extraordinary manifestations of divine power are stronger in their faith than the miracle-seekers, because they don't need miracles to believe. 'Blessed are those who have not seen and who yet believe' said Our Lord.

Incidentally, Hinn is also interesting in another connection. He was a disciple of celebrated American healing crusade leader Kathryn Kuhlman, who died in 1976. Although he did affiliate to the Assemblies of God briefly, he now has his own 'Interdenominational Church', which is a very confusing term. Such churches are founded by individuals who imagine that they are a means of avoiding identification with any particular existing denomination, although in reality they do of course represent a new denomination.

The Catholic Church and Faith healing

According to Catholic teaching, grace *perfects* nature and does not destroy it. This Catholic doctrine suggests that God's normal way is to endow our natural faculties with divine grace, so uplifting them and embellishing them, rather than breaking into the natural order and doing outwardly spectacular actions. So the skilled and accomplished surgeon's work is also a sign of God's grace. Many converts to Catholicism could testify to the release of fresh natural talents and gifts that ensued on their conversion.

This is not to deny that miracles – interruptions of the ordinary procedures of nature – occur, far from it. The Church has confirmed for example a number of healing miracles that took place at Lourdes, after careful medical investigation. But the Church does not place such things at the heart of her life and worship. Except that as a matter of fact the Mass is itself a miracle on the Catholic understanding, since we receive Christ under the veil of the host, and so, it could be argued, is the very existence of the Church across the world in so many cultures, languages, races, and climes, and yet with one common liturgy, one set of principles of living, one centre and one leader.

There is moreover as we have seen a dark side to the Miracle Crusades of evangelists like Benny Hinn and others. Evidence has been produced that on occasion in such events the sick may be sifted before they can get to the stage and physically prevented from going forward, so that the chronically ill or handicapped are kept away. It is known that there are individuals who do not get healed at all at the hands of such evangelists, while apparently instantaneous healings may often turn out to be temporary.

For some however this is not an argument against the Miracle Crusades, it means only that their faith is deficient. Such individuals may return again and again in hopes of healing. Yet this can be a deeply discouraging conclusion: 'I have not been healed, therefore my faith is not strong enough:' what this means is that thenceforth, on top of the affliction laid on me by the Good Lord for his mysterious purposes, I now feel guilty for having that affliction.

Catholic tradition teaches us to take our sufferings as a school for growth in grace, not to fight against them as though they were a challenge to the weakness of our faith. This does not mean that we cannot pray for healing, far from it. What it means is that we learn to see our afflictions in a positive light, for the gifts they contain.

St John of the Cross says that sufferings are the windows of the soul through which God enters our hearts. Not the only windows, of course he may come through joy too; but we don't usually need help to cope with joy, joy doesn't make us doubt God's love for us – whereas the experience of suffering can all too easily drive us away from God, unless we are taught how to handle it.

The global spread of Pentecostalism

Although Pentecostalism was already a sizeable phenomenon in the US and elsewhere between the Wars, the name of Aimee Semple McPherson being among the best known of its exponents, its dramatic global expansion has in fact taken place since the end of World War II. Since the 1960s a bewildering variety of Pentecostalist movements and denominations have spread all over the world and now have a very visible presence on TV. The main denominational affiliations are Assemblies of God and Elim churches, but there are innumerable others.

The largest single church in the world

The largest single church in the world based on one location in terms of numbers is a Yoido Full Gospel Church in Seoul, South Korea (claiming to have a regular worship attendance of over 800,000). Its growth was overseen by Pastor David Yonggi Cho, who started a tent church in 1958. Hundreds of assistant pastors and thousands of cell group leaders help run the organisation, with the majority being women. The term 'full gospel' is commonly used by Pentecostalists to refer to the way that the doctrine of the Baptism of the Holy Spirit 'completes' the traditional gospel message.

Latin America

All over Latin America Pentecostal sects are spreading at massive speed, usually at the expense of the Catholic Church. There are said to be 75 million Pentecostalists currently in the Continent. Some of the adherents have a high public profile, like the Brazilian footballer Kaka. One recent estimate claimed that 85% of Brazilian Protestants are Pentecostalists, and they have in recent times started to emerge as a force in national life.

The home church of the Brazil para Cristo ('Brazil for Christ') movement is said to accommodate as many as 30,000; this building is in São Paulo and officially seats 15,000. Also in São Paulo, the Deus é Amor ('God is Love') church has an official 10,000 capacity but is often overcrowded. It is estimated that there are 24 million Pentecostalists in Brazil (the largest number in any country in the world) as compared with 5.8 million in the USA.

The Universal Church of the Kingdom of God is said to control seventy television and more than fifty radio stations as well as a number of newspapers. Annual 'Marches for Jesus' organised by all the country's Pentecostal churches have been known to attract more than two million.

At one time Pentecostalism was regarded as a reactionary force in Latin American politics, but there is evidence that this opinion is outdated. Its adherents seem to thrive in the slums and provide something that the poor are seeking. Worshippers dress soberly and are offered hope of escape from addictions and the chance to begin a new life. Left-wing regimes in Bolivia and Venezuela actively court the Pentecostalist vote. In Mexico they are well represented among the poor of the Chiapas region.

It is not unknown however in Latin America for individuals to attend Catholic mass as well as going to Pentecostal churches, and to come for Catholic baptism for their infants.

Africa

In Africa Pentecostalism is rampant. One estimate claims that ten percent of Africa's population was 'Charismatic' at the start of the third millennium. The message of Azusa Street was brought to Africa very quickly.

The picture is very complex but there is in Africa a type of independent church known as a 'Spirit church' which is not the same as Pentecostal but which does stress healing, prophecy, and the gift of tongues. One authority states that 'such a fundamental change has taken place in African Christianity that Pentecostalism has become its dominant expression in many countries'. Large-scale immigration from Africa to the UK has brought this style of religion with it to the British Isles.

In African Pentecostalism the role of demons and exorcism is particularly pervasive. Revival meetings and open-air services often culminate in ceremonies of the casting out of demons.

Britain

In Britain the Pentecostalist movement has never attained the kind of critical mass to be found in the USA or in some of the Latin American countries. For a long time the Kensington Temple in London was the best-known Pentecostalist church in England. It was originally founded in 1849 by a group of Congregationalists but sold in 1931 to the Elim Foursquare Gospel Alliance. It attracts many thousands of worshippers on a Sunday both to its main building and to 'satellite' centres elsewhere. Elim Pentecostal churches is an umbrella movement that claims the adherence of 500 congregations in the UK and a presence in forty countries around the world.

A number of small chains of Pentecostal congregations appeared in the UK in the late twentieth century. They include the Bugbrooke community whose evangelistic arm, the Jesus Army, has between 50 and 80 branches; Cornerstone Ministries with 35 or so congregations, Covenant Ministries International with 35; the Ichthus Fellowship founded by Roger and Faith Forster with more than 25 congregations. New Frontiers International claims around 200 congregations. Pioneer's leader, Gerald Coates, has a high profile as an evangelical leader, but it is however geographically restricted to Southeast England.

Pentecostalism has been particularly influential amongst immigrants to the UK from Africa and the West

Indies, and the largest single congregation in the country is said to be the Kingsway International Christian Centre based in East London and pastored by Nigerian-born Matthew Ashimowolo. It claims to have grown from 300 Sunday worshippers at its foundation in 1992 to 12,000 today. The membership is said to be predominantly West African. There are satellite churches in other locations.

United States

In the United States the largest and strongest white Pentecostalist denomination is the Assemblies of God, which began in 1914 as a fellowship of Pentecostal ministers who saw in collaborative action a means of advancing shared objectives. Some Pentecostalists did not welcome this; an influential strand in the movement thought that the New Testament did not offer any grounds for anything more than local church order, a way of thinking which has long antecedents.

The International Church of the Foursquare Gospel founded by celebrated evangelist Aimee Semple Mcpherson in 1923 had affiliated to it by the beginning of the third millennium more than 1250 churches in the US and more than 15,000 worldwide. Global membership was claimed to be over one million.

A well-known movement for laypersons is the Full Gospel Businessmens' Fellowship founded by Demos

Shakarian, whose forebears had fled Armenia in advance of massacres as a result of a warning from a Pentecostal prophet. The Fellowship is particularly known for its prayer breakfasts for businessmen.

The Church of God based in Cleveland has more than one and a half million members worldwide and has a history of interracialism with many black ministers. The Church of God of Prophecy is an offshoot from it. This denomination lays a particular emphasis on worship services not only on Sundays but in the week. It too has a high degree of racial integration with many racially mixed congregations. It has a significant presence in the UK where however it is seen as a black church.

There are smaller Pentecostal denominations in the US too numerous to mention, such as the Pentecostal Church of God with nearly 5000 churches outside the US as well as more than 1200 at home and a worldwide membership of 600,000.

The 'Latter Rain Movement'

Historically an important part in the development of Pentecostalism after World War II was played by the 'Latter Rain Movement' in the US, which essentially replayed much of the original excitement with 'supernatural' phenomena such as tongues-speaking and prophecy and healing that was characteristic of the Azusa Street Revival of forty years earlier. It produced one curious teaching according to which the Old Testament Feast of Passover and the Feast of Pentecost having found fulfilment, the Feast of Tabernacles, the third of Israel's great feasts, had yet to be fulfilled. Another substantial movement within Pentecostalism (particularly in the US) has been the Oneness Movement, which believes that baptism should be in the name of Jesus only, and not in the name of the Blessed Trinity.

'Third Wave'

Finally, reference needs to be made to the term 'Third Wave', which reflects the chaotic situation of today in which there are not only Pentecostalists (first wave) in their own specific denominations and Charismatics (second wave) within the denominations but a movement whose members are positive about the work of the Holy Spirit as seen in the first two waves without wishing to identify themselves with either. This is in part because the use of terms like 'Charismatic' or 'Spirit-filled' is seen as dangerously divisive and there is a preference for making compromises seen as necessary for the preservation of unity; also because these terms might seem to imply the existence of a kind of spiritual elite.

The reluctance to use Pentecostal terminology is characteristic of a wide variety of modern 'Neocharismatics' who belong to congregations or communities where there is an emphasis on the Holy

Spirit and spiritual gifts, signs and wonders. Such congregations have proliferated in recent years all over the world, many of them being classed as 'postdenominational' because they think they can escape being tied to a denomination.

The 'Word of Faith' movement

An increasingly popular and prominent current within Pentecostalism is the Word of Faith or Word-Faith Movement, which espouses the 'prosperity doctrine', also known as 'Positive Confession Theology' or 'faith-formula theology'. This involves the notion that we can 'claim the promises of God' in the sense that we can ask God for whatever it is that we want and He will give it to us.

'The prosperity gospel'

If a person truly believes and asks God for a new car or a house or even a plane, then God will give him that. Prosperity is actually a divine right. It is often known as 'the prosperity gospel' and is frequently denounced not only by other Evangelicals but by those Pentecostalists who regard it as heretical.

The preachers of this doctrine themselves are liable to demonstrate their credentials via their own affluence, which has led to American Congressional inquiries in some cases.

From a Catholic perspective this looks like the very opposite of the teaching of Jesus, who lived and died a poor man and exhorted his followers to let go of the things of this world if they wanted to save their souls. Pastor David Yonggi Cho, founder of the Yoido Full Gospel Church in Seoul which was mentioned earlier as being the world's largest single congregation, is a prominent exponent of the prosperity gospel.

Illness as lack of faith

The movement has also adopted a belief that seems to owe its origins to New Thought in the USA and to Christian Science, that illness is never willed by God and that we can conquer it by faith. This causes a great deal of anger not simply amongst Evangelical observers, but also among some other Pentecostalists. It is particularly painful for persons who pray devoutly for healing without receiving it. They are prone to attribute the absence of healing to a lack of faith on their part, and this means that on top of the suffering they already endure from the illness, they may be tormented by a sense of guilt as well.

One of the early pioneer figures in the Word of Faith movement, named William Marrion Branham, lost his wife and baby in 1937 when he was 28 years old, and he attributed this to an act of disobedience on his part to a divine call.

Assessing Pentecostalism

In the last decades of the twentieth century ecstatic phenomena such as tongues-speaking gradually became more acceptable within the established denominations, and individuals could now remain within their denominations while carrying the new label 'Charismatic'.

Pentecostalism and the Charismatic Movement

It is very important to distinguish between 'Pentecostalist' and 'Charismatic'. Generally speaking, we can say that while Pentecostalists operate in movements for which the stress on baptism in the Spirit and tongues-speaking with associated ecstatic phenomena are standard, central, and 'normal' in belief and practice, Charismatics operate within movements and denominations where the stress on baptism in the Spirit and tongue-speaking with associated ecstatic phenomena set them apart from their peers as a particular movement within their church or community.

So it is with Charismatics in the Catholic Church. The Charismatic Movement is not the Catholic Church but a movement within the Catholic Church, it is indeed one of many movements within the Church which represent different emphases of spirituality (eg Ignatian, Franciscan, Carmelite, etc). The Charismatic Movement then represents a focus on miraculous aspects of the Christian life within the mainline and other churches, while Pentecostalists makes these the heart and foundation of their creed, worship, and practice.

The Charismatic Movement as ecumenical

The Charismatic Movement has been ecumenical from the start, it has frequently involved ecumenical prayer gatherings or worship services. The Pentecostal Movement as it developed more than fifty years before the Charismatic Movement was a movement within Protestantism which involved the founding of new breakaway communities and sects based on 'Pentecostalist' principles.

Dennis Bennett

The Charismatic Movement as a focus on tongues-speaking and miraculous phenomena as witnessed in the Early Church is generally considered to have originated in 1959 with the activities of Dennis Bennett, parish priest of a Californian Episcopalian parish, who wrote about his experiences of 'baptism in the Spirit' in a bestselling book entitled *Nine o'clock in the Morning*.

What was new about Bennett was that as an Episcopalian he belonged not to the Evangelical wing of

Protestantism but to the High Church movement within the Anglican Communion, whose liturgical and other beliefs owed as much to those of the Catholic Church as to those of Anglicanism. Having experienced 'the baptism of the Spirit' Bennett moreover remained in his denomination rather than joining a Pentecostal denomination or even starting a new one himself.

This marked the moment when a Charismatic movement began to spread within the Episcopalian Church and come to wider public attention. Although there were precedents in other American denominations and in the Episcopal Church itself where individuals began to exercise the charismatic gifts, it was Bennett's experience and the publicity surrounding it that gave the major impetus.

The Charismatic Movement within Catholocism

The Charismatic movement within Catholicism emerged a decade or so later in the USA among students at Duquesne University (1967), and it soon became an officially-authorised spiritual way in the Catholic Church. It is usually referred to within the Church as the 'Charismatic Renewal' movement or just as the 'Renewal'.

The term 'Charismatic' is derived from the Greek word for the 'gifts' (charismata) of the Holy Spirit. (This use of the term with a capital C is to be distinguished from its general traditional use to refer to someone who possesses unusual gifts for attracting the attention, enthusiasm, and support of others.) St Paul speaks about these gifts in 1 Corinthians 12, 4-11. He says that the gifts are shared out among believers, each with a different one.

The list of these gifts includes preaching with wisdom, faith, healing, miracle working, prophecy, recognition of spirits, tongues and the ability to interpret them. 'All these are the work of one and the same Spirit, who distributes different gifts to different people just as he chooses' (1 Cor 12, 11). It does seem clear from these verses that the gift of tongues is one of several gifts and that each believer normally majors in one of the gifts, so the verses cannot be used to justify any claim that all believers should expect to speak in tongues or to have the gift of healing, for example.

Still, Charismatics and Pentecostalists assume that any believer can expect to receive from God gifts such as tongues-speaking, prophecy, interpretation of prophecy, exhortation or encouragement, etc. A Charismatic mass may therefore include tongues-speaking and Catholic Charismatic meetings are held where the gifts are exercised.

On the question of tongues-speaking and on the wider question of the individual believer's right to lay claim to this gift for himself or herself there is then agreement between Pentecostalists and Catholic Charismatics. But of course Catholic Charismatics remain obedient to Mother Church and in communion with Rome and subject to the normal disciplines of the Catholic Church.

Protestants and Catholics not involved in the Charismatic movement do not share the same expectation of receiving these supernatural spiritual gifts and do not focus on them in the same way as Pentecostalists and Charismatic Catholics. Whereas the Charismatic Movement is respected and authorised within the Catholic Church, mainstream Protestants are often somewhat suspicious of tongues-speaking and the gifts of the Spirit.

The question of the place of the miraculous in the 'normal' Christian life is the focus of a long history in controversy. In the medieval Church healing miracles were sought and expected – perhaps in consequence of the absence of any adequate medical science. After the Reformation the Catholic Church continued to experience the miraculous and the nineteenth and twentieth centuries in particular were replete with extraordinary phenomena such as Marian Apparitions in various places, the stories associated with the Miraculous Medal, and the appearance of St Pio of Pietrelcina, associated with numerous miraculous occurrences.

Head or heart

Meanwhile the Protestant denominations tended to move in one of two directions: either towards an 'official' church mentality in the established churches of Northern Europe, in which the cerebral element in religion, or head knowledge, was uppermost, or, largely in rebellion against this, towards a religion of the heart and the emotions in which evidences and proofs of God's action in the world were actively sought. One of the best-known movements embodying this latter approach was Pietism which arose in Germany and saw itself as supremely a 'religion of the heart'. It was this kind of religion, exported to America, that provided the soil out of which Pentecostalism would emerge.

The place of miracles

The Pentecostal Movement raises in acute form the question of the place of miracles in the life of the Church. Pentecostalists base their understanding of the Christian faith on the assumption that the miracles experienced by the Early Church should be the birthright of every believer. The principle is at first sight an attractive and challenging one, but the issue is a much more complex one than Pentecostals make out.

A model in the past

The first thing to be considered is that there is always a danger in looking back to a model in the past – even when that past is the amazing past of the Early Church. The whole history of Protestantism since the Reformation has been disfigured and distorted by arguments and divisions over how to recover the life experienced by the first Christians and recorded in the Book of Acts.

At the extreme the end result is sects like the Amish who literally refuse every technological product of modernity almost completely or like the Quakers who sit together waiting for the Pentecostal spirit to fall or the Plymouth Brethren, who dispense with an ordained ministry entirely. There is a massive historical connection between the urge to recover the lifestyle and the experiences of the first Christians and fissiparity or relentless fragmentation of the body of believers into competing sects.

In the case of the Catholic Church, it may be argued that the purity of the early Christian understanding of the Spirit-filled life has been maintained above all in the religious orders – though some would perhaps point to the New Movements in more recent times.

The second important point is that the experiences and the life of the first Christians is portrayed not only in the Book of Acts but also in the Epistles; and even a cursory reading of St Paul's First Letter to the Corinthians for example reveals that there was quite another side to the life of the first Christian communities, which were also prone to divisions – some for Paul, some for Apollos etc -and to massive moral failings – a man living with his stepmother, the assembly failing to subject the couple to the proper discipline, and believers taking disputes among themselves to the secular courts.

It is hopeless to imagine that the purity of the community described in the Book of Acts can be preserved without the human failings found among believers, and yet it has often been because of perceived moral failings that modern Pentecostal groups have fragmented; they are all too prone to tear each other apart in the quest for a pure church permanently lit up by the power of the Spirit.

The Catholic faithful have a protection from this in the common obedience to the Magisterium, which makes the concept of a fellowship not in communion with the Pope unacceptable. However, individual Catholics do in fact from time to time abandon the Mother Church for Pentecostalism, disappointed perhaps that she herself does not in their view seem to manifest the power of the Spirit sufficiently.

Miracles in the Catholic Church

This brings us onto the question of miracles and the Power of the Spirit. Debate over the place of Pentecost and its accompanying miracles in the continuing life of the Church has a long history. Catholic apologists employed against the Protestant Reformers the polemical argument that the latter could not lay claim to any miracles.

This argument draws attention to the fact that the Catholic Church was therefore assumed to be a place where miracles did occur. And in fact in the lives of the

Catholic saints we see numerous accounts of miracles right down to modern times: St Bernadette for example saw Our Lady at Lourdes, and a stream which gushed from the ground near the place of apparition later became associated with miracles of healing. In the twentieth century St Pio (Padre Pio) was reportedly responsible for many miracles, not to mention the permanent miracle that he carried the stigmata – the wounds of Christ – on his hands and on his feet in a manner inexplicable to medical science.

Miracles have in fact remained a central part of the Catholic faith, and indeed the Church herself is a standing miracle, for she represents the largest single voluntary movement on the face of the planet, and yet she possesses an extraordinary unity; her members follow the same faith and accept the same doctrine and moral teaching whether they live in Africa, Asia, America, or Europe. A Catholic can go to mass anywhere in the world and it will be essentially the same mass though in a different language, and the catechism of doctrine will be the same.

Even the notorious moral failings of certain popes of the past – or indeed at one particularly dark period, the existence of multiple rival popes - did nothing to corrupt the faith of the Church. This does seem to be nothing short of a miracle, and there is certainly nothing else like it in existence. Finally, in the process of beatification by which the Church declares someone a Saint, a crucial part is played by properly validated miracles associated with requests for help to that saint.

By contrast, miracles have not sat well with the established Protestant denominations like Anglicanism or the Lutheran state churches, and the point made by Catholic apologists in this regard was not lost at different times on Protestants themselves, who have been all too prone to look for them outside the confines of the denominations and eventually to collaborate in the establishment of movements for which they were fundamental.

Confusion around divine healing

Unfortunately, there is a great deal of confusion about the whole question of divine healing among Christians today – including Catholics. The Mother Church has always exercised extreme caution in relation to alleged 'miraculous' healings, requiring passage of time and the official testimony of medical experts when it comes to such healings in connection with canonisations.

It is often forgotten in church circles that the devil can perform healing miracles too. Someone who carried out a great deal of research in this area was Lutheran Pastor Kurt Koch, who found himself counselling many individuals suffering from psychic or mental disturbances and who came to a remarkable conclusion: that when 'healing' came from a satanic rather than the divine power, the disease did not in fact disappear but merely shifted to another location in that person's being – all too often it entered the person's psyche instead of their body.

There is another point to be made about miracles. It is evident from the Gospels that in performing his miracles Our Lord was very concerned that people would follow him not because of the extraordinary feats he performed. Frequently he exhorted those present to tell nobody. The great Catholic saints likewise did not trumpet their miracles – whether St Pio or St Teresa of Avila or whoever, and for the same reason. Moreover, it is no accident that when Our Lord healed the ten lepers, only one came back to thank him. Miracles of healing do not necessarily lead to a change of heart.

One of the most sobering of all the sayings in the Scripture is the story of the beggar Lazarus and the rich man Dives. Lazarus was taken to heaven after his life of suffering while Dives ended up being tortured by fire as a punishment for his indifference during his earthly life. Dives wanted to get through to those like him on earth but was told that 'even if one were to rise from the dead, they would not believe'.

Undue focus on miracles

This cannot however diminish the force of the fact that the birth of the Church at Pentecost was accompanied by an extraordinary outpouring of miracles. What it does tell us is that even a miracle-a-minute church life would not necessarily bring multitudes of individuals closer to God, because miracles do not necessarily have the power of boosting faith that is attributed to them.

In fact the thirst for miracles is not a sign that we are taking our faith especially seriously, as some seem to think, it is on the contrary a sign of weak faith. Strong faith does not need miracles because, as St John of the Cross observed, it holds out its hand in the dark and hangs on to the hand of God. True love for God loves in the teeth of suffering and pain and heartache. Do we want God for himself, or for the goodies that he may give us?

The New Testament itself holds out warnings against an undue focus on miracles. On a famous occasion when ten lepers were healed by Jesus, only one came back to thank him – an episode which is profoundly instructive. When he healed Bartimaeus, he followed it up not by saying 'Your faith has restored your sight to you' but 'Your faith has saved you'.

Ultimately Jesus came to save souls, it is the soul which is the essential part of us humans, he came to bring the gift of eternal life, it is a gift which he tells us is available to anybody of any age and class and caste and race, irrespective of the individual's physical health or otherwise. He did not come to turn humans into a physically perfect species but to teach us how to cope productively and cheerfully with our burdens, ailments, and disabilities. For that healing of the soul is what we need above all.

Could it be that the cult of healing within Pentecostalism might be connected with our civilisation's obsession about physical perfection?

Informality in Pentecostalism

There are two features of the spirit of Pentecostalism which have a great attraction today, particularly among the young and impressionable: I am thinking of its informality and its theatricality.

Informality is a characteristic of the evangelical movement in general, from which Pentecostalism inherits many features. Prescribed liturgy and ritual is widely associated with the Catholic Church and with the established Protestant churches, and in the postwar era this kind of formal worship has been increasingly regarded as a practice destructive of the freedom of the Spirit.

The reaction in the postwar West to the experience of the totalitarian dictatorships inspired a huge veneration for the idea of freedom, which was one of the fundamental features of the great youth movements of the 1960s which are particularly associated with '68 – the student movement, the hippies, the rejection of traditions of formal clothing in favour of jeans and shorts and even the abandonment of footwear, the spread of informal forms of address and the widespread use of Christian names etc. This freedom was widely identified with individualism and 'doing your own thing'; the slogan 'tune in and drop out' was symptomatic of an attitude of rejection of established institutions and formalities.

Inevitably this spirit affected religion; Evangelicals were quite ready to abandon formal liturgical gowns or robes, allow rock bands instead of the more formal organ or piano, and adopt contemporary informal language in their worship services.

Although the spirit did also affect the Catholic Church, where 'trendy' clerics might wear their hair long or abandon priestly garb and allow informal folk masses, the Catholic liturgy as something inherited cannot be individualised in the same way and there are other barriers inherent in Catholicism to an understanding of freedom which cuts the present off from the past.

Theatricality in Pentecostalism

The typical American Pentecostal preacher (eg Roy Fields, the Florida outpouring) appears on stage in informal attire and speaks the colloquial language of his audience. (It is still usually a 'he', female preachers are rare – though Joyce Meyer and Aimee Semple McPherson are powerful exceptions.) The appearance of Roy Fields is more startling than most – he is copiously adorned with tattoos and wears T-shirts and jeans and wanders around the stage constantly as he speaks. The typical Pentecostal Evangelist engages with his audience in a manner very similar to that of the TV chat shows or even the comedians. This brings us to the second feature of Pentecostalism that attracts many younger impressionable persons today: its theatricality.

Pentecostalism makes for great melodrama and showbiz. Like showbiz, it is of course therefore highly vulnerable to manipulation and is riddled with personality cults. More than a few televangelists with a cult following have turned out to have feet of clay and have been subjected to public exposure, the most famous examples being former US Assemblies of God ministers Jim Bakker and Jimmy Swaggart. Evangelical movements have always been tempted down the road of the personality cult, but Pentecostalism even more so.

Whereas in the traditional broader evangelical movement the celebrated preacher figure – such as Billy Graham - is known almost exclusively for his power to persuade and convince of the truth of the Bible and the need for individuals to submit their lives to Christ, the Pentecostal preacher is known for his ability to conjure up extraordinary phenomena.

A meeting in which individuals come up for healing or claim healing will inevitably generate a sense of drama, as will a meeting in which highly visual occurrences take place such as individuals falling to the ground at the touch of the pastor's fingertip (or even when the fingertip is pointed in their direction), or individuals being completely engulfed with laughter, or speaking in tongues. The atmosphere of expecting the unexpected makes for huge dramatic tension and excitement.

It has been argued that this excitement is one of the reasons why Pentecostalism is attractive to the urban poor in Latin America, where there may be very little in the way of entertainment available. In contrast the Catholic mass is known in advance and the action is largely internal to the heart and mind of the priest and the participant. As a matter of fact, to the eye of faith the mass is itself a huge miracle, since the Church teaches that Christ is actually and individually consumed by each person who consumes the host.

Why are the Pentecostals so successful?

Given the massive global spread of this religion, it is natural to ask what factors lie behind it. Why does this religion seem to have such a universal appeal today? Many answers have been offered to this question. Sociologists have grappled with specific situations in places like South Korea or Brazil.

In the former case, it seems that Pentecostalism has managed to adapt certain practices prevalent in the traditional religion, and indeed some commentators consider the religion of preachers like David Yonggi Cho to be nothing more than a Christianised Shamanism.

Latin American Pentecostalists on the other hand seem to have taken up the idea of the option for the poor proclaimed in Catholic circles in the 1960s. Originally identified with the forces of political conservatism, they have now developed welfare programmes and a whole panoply of social concern activities.

Mainstream

At a deeper level, it looks as though there may be more substantive issues at stake. I spent ten years of my own life as an Evangelical Protestant, and one of the themes of this kind of thinking in the 1960s was that it was 'countercultural'. Instead of the soft culture of drugs, promiscuity, and life experience as the goal and end of everything, it offered a hard-edged culture of self-discipline and a readiness to serve ideals in the interests of the gift of eternal life.

We believed that our attractiveness to young people – which was very real – lay in our confident proclamation of this countercultural message. But over the years I became convinced that the reality was very different. What made us attractive was not that we stood for different values than those of the decadent 60s, but that apart from our moral emphases, we were all too much a part of the mainstream.

We were enthusiastic about rock music put to the service of the gospel and 'Christian' bands proliferated among us. We were desperately keen to communicate in a 'modern' way, using visual images, drama, and music to communicate our message. In a parish I served in once in my days as an Evangelical minister, we held special evangelistic services aimed at winning outsiders to the Gospel, handing out tickets for our members to pass on to their friends and acquaintances. It was at this point that I began to ponder the Catholic mass and the fact that people seemed to go to mass week by week even though it was essentially the same, they did not need incentives like special music or visiting celebrity speakers or dramatic interludes etc. This led me to the sobering reflection that in some way we were trying to attract people to the church by entertaining them.

Here lies the link with Pentecostalism. Is it legitimate to ask how important in Pentecostalism is the entertainment quotient? Although these services follow a simple basic pattern of singing plus bible reading plus prayer plus preacher, they also hold a promise of excitement, of the unexpected, of the spectacular even: who will be healed this week? Will people fall on the floor, will they start to bark, will they break out into tongues?

Spontaneity

This craving for the unexpected, for drama in fact, this theatrical aspect of Pentecostalism, is connected with a very important principle that holds good in the minds of many modern persons. Traditional denominations, as I said earlier, hold to simple worship structures in their weekly services. At most among evangelicals there would be some scope for extempore prayer. But Evangelicals do not really do liturgy beyond that because they associate the Holy Spirit with the idea of freedom from the constraints of ritual, of set liturgy. To follow a set service or a printed book in your worship is already anathema to many Evangelicals, for they associate the presence of the Spirit with spontaneity. Again, this association is typical of the mood which emerged in the 60s, a mood which has persisted strongly in our Western cultures.

We can see it operative in education, for example, where rote learning of information, which is still practised in schools in places like China, came to be seen as somehow 'anti-humanistic'. 'Real' education meant spontaneous dialogue between students and teacher, it meant teachers tailoring their lessons to the needs of their particular group of pupils, etc.

The same spirit can be seen in music, where in place of the sober-suited sedentary orchestra you have the rock band members leaping about all over the stage and occasionally shouting or even screaming into the microphone. In place of sedate ballroom dancing you have the mad gyrations of couples which basically all follow the rhythm of the music while each couple 'does their own thing'.

This association of the work of the Spirit with spontaneity is powerful in the Pentecostalist movements, and it is why for many of them the Catholic Church, following her year-round routine of set liturgies, looks to be hostile to the work of the Spirit.

Catholics and Pentecostalism

From its inception the Catholic Charismatic Movement has followed an ecumenical pattern in its prayer groups and this has helped to break down fears of the Catholic Church in some sectors of Protestantism.

The Catholic Charismatic Movement is held fully within the Mother Church and is approved by her. The maternal care of the Church makes it possible to check and restrain the potentially wild and misguided emotions and behaviours that often accompany the infusion of what are felt as spiritual gifts and blessings.

Leading figures in the Church from the time of Cardinal Suenens on have patronised and encouraged the Movement, as did Pope John Paul II. During his reign the Preacher to the Papal Household, Fr Raniero Cantalamessa, identified prominently with it. Numerous books and articles have been published by such persons in support of the charismatic position.

Catholics obviously need to distinguish between the exercise of the charismatic gifts of the Spirit within the protective sphere of grace of the Mother Church and their exercise in the Pentecostalist and Neo-Pentecostalist setting. The late Cardinal Suenens of Malines-Brussels was a powerful advocate of the Charismatic movement in the Church.

Mystical ecstasy

The Catholic tradition is replete with cases of mystical ecstasy: for example St Teresa of Avila, who was actually seen to levitate by her fellow nuns. Nearer to our own time it is recorded of Padre Pio – now St Pio of Pietrelcina – that during his masses in his younger days he sometimes fell into trances so profound that his masses could last five hours. The simple farmers who came had to ask the bishop to be dispensed from staying the full length since they all had much work to do.

In St Teresa's equally-mystically inclined confrere, St John of the Cross, we find a warning that we are to seek God rather than excitement or emotional uplift. St Teresa made it clear that her mystical experiences were not what the life of faith and discipleship was all about, and she tells us that she spent eighteen years in joyless and unrewarded prayer before experiencing anything.

It could be argued that this was and is ultimately the real goal of the charismatic experience – to achieve a kind of state of ecstasy in which the self is forgotten along with the normal boundaries of our existence like time and space and the frameworks that condition our lives. This corresponds to the kind of experience sought in the secular world through drugs or through immersion in meditation. The aim for the individual is to forget himself or herself.

Looked at from this point of view, it may seem unsurprising that the Pentecostal impulse appeared with greatly renewed force in the twentieth century and indeed that it has continued to grow unstoppably into the third millennium.

Understanding the
New Age Movement

The New Age Movement is regarded by many
Christians as a growing threat to traditional beliefs and
practices. Why are so many people attracted to
astrology, reincarnation and
magic, to spiritualism and
goddess-worship, to new cults
and old heresies? This clear and
thoroughly researched text
explores the meaning and
direction of the New Age
Movement in relation to
Catholic teaching, and asks
how Catholics can best
respond to the challenge it
represents. Stratford Caldecott is the author of
Catholic Social Teaching: A Way In.

CTS Explanations is a series explaining in everyday
language Catholic teaching on a range of current
pressing moral and ethical issues.

ISBN: 978 186082 408 1

CTS Code: Ex 23

Protestantism

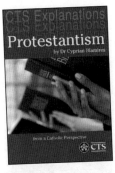

Protestants account for just under half of all Christians in the world but are often placed in opposition to the other Catholic half. This booklet explores the roots of this split and the political and theological differences which caused it. It also looks at modern day Protestantism, identifying the main distinctions within it and how these relate to Catholic Christianity.

Cyprian Blamires was ordained to the Anglican ministry after reading theology at Oxford. He was recieved into the Catholic Church in 1979 and subsequently obtained an Oxford doctorate in history.

ISBN: 978 1 86082 432 6

CTS Code: Ex 24

Mormons
The Church of Jesus Christ of Latter-day Saints

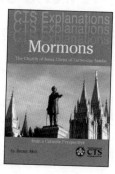

The Church of Jesus Christ of Latter-day Saints now claims over 12 million members world wide. This booklet describes Mormonism's core beliefs and whether they can truly claim to be Christian. Fundamental differences between the Catholic Faith and that held by Mormons are explored and advice given on how to engage in sincere and respectful dialogue with missionaries one can meet in many places across the world.

Jimmy Akin is the Director of Apologetics and Evangelization at Catholic Answers (*www.catholic.com*) and the author of the books *Mass Confusion: The Do's and Don'ts of Catholic Worship* and *The Salvation Controversy*, as well as numerous articles and other publications.

ISBN: 978 1 86082 439 5

CTS Code: Ex 25